BY DARYL KRAFT

Ten verses that can

change forever

how you see

God and the

Christian life

Cover design and illustrations by Debby Dahlke, Coeur d'Alene, Idaho.

Knowing the God Who Chose You
By Daryl Kraft
ISBN 0-9740109-0-1
Library of Congress Catalog Card Number: 2003106034

Copyright © 2003 by Daryl Kraft

Published by:
It's About Lives Ministries
P.O. Box 3108
Hayden, ID 83835-3108

www.itsaboutlives.org

Printed in the United States of America
All Rights Reserved.

To Mark, for the idea that inspired this book;
To Allyson, for painstakingly choosing the right words;
And most especially to Sherryl, for the ever-faithful prayers
and loving, wise counsel that made it all possible.

Table of Contents

Part Two: NEW LIFE ~ NEW FREEDOMS

INTRODUCTION TO A WHOLE NEW GOD

Looking back over my years as a Christian, I feel I have lived two distinct lives, as if midway through those years, I actually died, then came back an entirely different person. The first half I spent more time fearing God than experiencing His love, often viewing Him like the picture on the Uncle Sam poster, with His finger pointing down at me, telling me I'd better obey Him, or He would strike me down with His big stick. My Christian life consisted of little more than trying to follow a rigid program of do's and don'ts. Yet, no matter how hard I tried, I felt I still fell short of being the Christ-like person God wanted me to be.

During that early time, I attempted to discipline myself to a regular study of God's Word, hoping if I just "applied" the right verses to my life, I would eventually become less angry, selfish, and critical, and would overcome my fear of what others thought of me. But the Christ-like qualities I was trying so hard to emulate never seemed to stick. They slipped off again and again, like Band-Aids™ in the shower, so that over time, I gradually fell victim to an ever-increasing skepticism about the so-called "life of faith."

How could I possibly live up to all God had done for me, I wondered? And as for witnessing to others about Christ—why would I want to try and sell them on something with which I myself was not totally comfortable? I mean, wasn't being a committed Christian just another way of saying you gave up most of the fun in life so you could live an odd-duck, boring, religious life, eventually go to some third-world country as a missionary, and then get eaten in the end by a big snake? Why would anybody want to go through all that, just to spend eternity wearing a halo and strumming a harp on some cloud?

At the same time, I was certain the alternative would be worse. So I spent a lot of time worrying whether my "salvation ticket" would be good enough to get me through the pearly gates. On occasion I would even awaken in a cold sweat in the dead of night wondering, *How can I ever possibly know—beyond the shadow of a doubt—that when I die, I'll really wake up in heaven?*

Then one day, my whole view of God and the Christian life began to change. I wasn't attending a psychology class or counseling session. I wasn't reading some popular self-help book. I simply came face to face with a completely different Lord than I had ever imagined—in the person of a dear, dying cousin: my childhood companion, David.

Seeing him on his deathbed, at age 34, surrounded by his wife and the young children who would grow up without his loving presence, I realized Dave possessed a *peace* which I had sought all my life and never found. He was on the verge of losing everything and yet enjoyed perfect contentment; I had what I and the world considered "success," yet was gulping down tranquilizers to cope with it.

Confronted that day by the profound and supernatural calm in my cousin's demeanor, I was shaken to the core and forced to admit: *I don't know the same Lord he does.* Desperate to meet this God who could give such peace to a dying man, I imagined unzipping my chest, reaching in with my right hand to take hold of my heart, then handing it up to God, all the time earnestly and silently praying, *Lord, the life I've been living is too heavy and painful to live anymore. I am desperate to know You and to experience the peace Dave has found in you. Please, Lord, take everything I am, everything I have, everything I value. Take my business, my title, whatever my success, my little material wealth. Take all the respect I've tried to gain, for I want to trade it all…just to know You.*

That was the beginning of a whole new life for me.

The first thing I noticed was that my fear of the big-stick, Uncle-Sam God had vanished. And whereas, up until that time, reading the Scriptures had been dry and burdensome, now verses seemed to jump off the page with new truth and life. Most importantly, as the Holy Spirit began to etch the meaning of those verses deep within my heart, I experienced the Lord Himself changing me—from the inside out—into the very person I had for so many painful years struggled unsuccessfully on my own to become. I was no longer striving to follow a list of religious do's and don'ts or focused on trying to be a "good Christian." Instead, the perfect and power-filled truth of God's Word was progressively setting me free from the binding chains of my "self"— my pride, anger, and bitterness, and the rigid self-imposed disciplines I had tried for so long to follow.

Of course, these changes didn't happen overnight. Twenty-four years have passed since the day I stood beside Dave in the hospital—and still I continue to grow in knowing the Lord. The ten brief reflections in this book offer only a small sampling of the countless verses that have brought His new life and freedom to me in that time. Nevertheless, I pray they will impress on your soul two very precious and powerful truths: first, that God is good—*all* good; and second, that He is willing and waiting at every moment to reveal Himself to you and me, whenever our whole desire is *simply to know Him.*

What does that mean for our lives? Well, when you get right down to it, it means life is incredibly simple! Because as long as our entire focus is on knowing Him alone, we can be assured the Lord Himself will direct us in every area and detail of our lives. He will flood our mind and heart with His thoughts, desires, and decisions. And He will move us, naturally and without stress, toward any disciplines and service to which He calls us.

So we don't have to waste our lives searching for the perfect formula or "how-to manual" of the Christian life.

And we don't have to hop from church to church or counselor to counselor trying to find peace and direction. God Himself is our Comforter and Lord, and that means we can go directly to Him with our hearts' most rending needs and questions and discover how faithful He is to take care of every detail in our lives.

Furthermore, we don't need to wait for an extraordinary experience, or search out a spiritual guru in order to guide us to God. All we have to do is say from the bottom of our hearts: *Lord, I don't want my own life anymore. I want Yours. I just want to **know You.***

Is that your desire, friend? If so, I hope you'll read on. Because whether you've been a Christian all your life, or are just now starting the journey, the God who chose you wants more than anything to reveal Himself to you.

And He's just waiting for you to want that, too.

Knowing
God
~
Knowing
Life

PART ONE

Knowing God

*…that I may
know Him
and the
power
of His
resurrection.*

CHAPTER 1

PHILIPPIANS 3:10

Knowing God

You Never Graduate

> *...that I may know
> Him and the
> power
> of His
> resurrection.*
>
> PHILIPPIANS 3:10

hat always strikes me about Philippians 3:10—and what continues to be life-changing for me even today—is that Paul, pouring out his heart's greatest desire here, doesn't write, "I want to serve Jesus," or "obey Him," or even "know more about Him." He simply declares, "I want to know *Him*." Paul's whole focus in this verse, in other words, isn't on the things he should be doing for the Lord. *It's on the Lord Himself.*

You see, Paul was confident that as long as his heart was set on knowing the Lord, obedience and service would be the natural manifestation of Christ's life growing in him. He therefore saw obeying and serving, not as duties *he* somehow needed to perform, but as the fruit *Christ* would bring to fullness—in him.

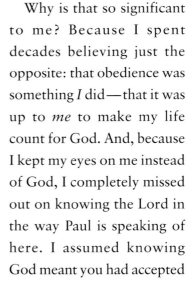

Because I kept my eyes on me, instead of God, I completely missed out on knowing the Lord the way Paul is speaking of here.

Why is that so significant to me? Because I spent decades believing just the opposite: that obedience was something *I* did—that it was up to *me* to make my life count for God. And, because I kept my eyes on me instead of God, I completely missed out on knowing the Lord in the way Paul is speaking of here. I assumed knowing God meant you had accepted Christ and the basic doctrines of the faith, but once you knew Him, you quickly graduated to showing your appreciation. How? By consulting God's "how-to manual"—the Bible—and trying to live accordingly.

So I witnessed to unbelievers at the office, remained faithful to my wife, and gave a portion of my income to charity. I became very active in my church and even taught a Sunday school class and served at times as an elder. I strove, in other words, to "live for the Lord," and, not surprisingly, was seen as a religious man.

What most people didn't know, however, was that deep inside I was miserable. The Lord I was trying so hard to "serve" was, as I envisioned, a stern, demanding God, poised to bring a big stick down on my head the moment I messed up in any way. Even though I knew the Scriptures taught that "God is Love," whenever I thought of Him reaching out His loving right hand to embrace me, I couldn't help recoiling from the club I imagined Him holding in His left. His standard of Christianity just seemed like an impossibly high benchmark He expected me to live up to—not to earn my salvation, but simply in return for what He had already done for me. I was constantly anxious about incurring His disapproval and worried that if I wasn't continually getting closer to that high standard, it might mean I wasn't truly saved.

From time to time, I'll admit, Paul's words about "knowing God" did give me pause. But I shrank back from the idea of getting any closer than necessary to the "big-stick" God of my imagination. How could just knowing more about Him make me a better person? And didn't committing more of one's life to God actually mean missing out on a lot of fun in this life anyway? What was so appealing about that?

Such thoughts kept me dangling in the breach, trying to serve and obey God enough to confirm in my own mind I was going to heaven, yet secretly fearing if I trusted too much of myself to Him, He would relegate me to a life of religious drudgery. And so I existed from year to year...until the day I stood by my dying cousin's bed and found myself wanting, more than anything in the world, to know the God who could give such peace to a dying man.

There, for the first time, I had to admit: *I didn't know the same God my cousin did.* I mean, how could I? I was taking up to six Valium a day just to cope with my life! At the same time, however, pondering the radiant calm on my cousin's face, I could sense a deep transformation stirring in my heart. For rather than wanting, as usual, to commit just enough of my life to the Lord to convince myself I was saved, I was beginning to feel a burning passion to experience His life-giving peace within my own heart.

In that instant, I cried out to the God I had never really known, with one single, all-consuming desire: that I might *know* Him. And in the very same moment, He began to reveal Himself to me—not as the sometimes loving, sometimes angry God I had for so long cowered before, but as an *all*-loving, *all*-compassionate Father who is ready to wrap me in His tender, healing embrace every time I turn to Him.

And as I've said before: that's when new life started.

Up to that moment, you see, the God I had always claimed to know and serve had been nothing more than a fabrication of the evil one. And Satan had kept me working so hard to please that warped image of God, that I never had the time or the inclination to draw closer to the True and Living Lord. But now I had encountered the resurrected Christ Himself, and over time He would begin to drive out the enemy's ugly distortions and lies with the perfect truth of His Word.

Of course, all those old lies didn't disappear overnight; liberation from the stress and weight of my former misconceptions continues even today. But as the Lord lovingly continues to close the gap between us, I am becoming more and more convinced that *knowing* Him is something quite different—and infinitely more wonderful—than just trying to live for Him.

Knowing Him is about growing in a relationship. It means actually feeling the joy and love of His presence with me and in me, and experiencing His thoughts, wisdom, and love guiding and changing me day by day, minute by minute. It is feeling every day as if I had just stepped out of my shoes and the Lord had stepped into them on my behalf.

But wait, you may say, doesn't knowing the Lord, first and foremost, mean living a life of obedience to the Lord?

What about all those New Testament exhortations, like "Be holy as I am holy"; "Prove yourselves doers of the Word"; and "Work out your own salvation with fear and trembling"? Didn't Jesus Himself say that if we loved Him, we would keep His commandments?

Knowing God is about growing in a relationship.

He most certainly did; and there can be no doubt that we are called to *walk in a manner worthy of the Lord, to please him in all respects, bearing fruit in every good work,* as Paul writes (Colossians 1:10). Furthermore, the New Testament is very plain in describing the details of such a walk. What we mustn't forget, however, is that the same God who tells us how to live as Christians just as clearly says that His commandments have no power to *enable* us to obey Him.

> *What the Law could not do, weak as it was through the flesh, God did: sending His own Son in the likeness of sinful flesh and as an offering for sin, He condemned sin in the flesh, so that the requirement of the Law might be fulfilled **in us**, who do*

*not walk according to the flesh but
according to the Spirit.*

Romans 8:3–4 (Emphasis added.)

While the countless exhortations of Jesus and the apostles do remind us what true righteousness looks like and expose areas where our self-life—our "flesh"—is still living and active, without Christ *in us* they are as utterly powerless to change us as the Old Testament law. That's why Jesus offered Himself for our sins, fulfilling the law in respect to our justification. We sometimes forget, however, that through His indwelling Spirit, He also *continues* to fulfill the law in terms of our sanctification as well.

*By His doing you are in Christ Jesus,
who became to us wisdom from God,
and righteousness **and sanctification,**
and redemption.*

1 Corinthians 1:30 (Emphasis added.)

Obedience—running the race—therefore, isn't about pulling ourselves up by the bootstraps to become better Christians; it's about totally trusting that the God who commands us to be holy is also the One who takes it upon Himself to make us that way!

*Let us run with endurance the race that
is set before us, fixing our eyes on Jesus,
the author **and perfecter** of faith.*

Hebrews 12:1–2 (Emphasis added.)

In fact, the astounding message of the Gospel is that
this very Lord is living within our hearts—*and He is the
perfect embodiment of every law and every exhortation
in all of Scripture!* So, as long as we are continuing to
surrender to His life in us—as long as our whole desire
is nothing more than to know and love Him—we can be
confident that *Jesus Himself* is already in the process of
fulfilling every one of God's commandments in our lives.

*It is God who is at work in you, both to
will and to work for His good pleasure.*

Philippians 2:13

That's why Paul could say that, in comparison to
knowing Christ, he considered everything else to be just
so much rubbish. He wasn't interested in flaunting his
spiritual pedigree or keeping track of how much he was
doing for the Lord. His consuming passion was purely
to commune with His Savior and to experience personally
everything that He is: unconditional love, joy, peace,
patience, kindness, goodness, faithfulness, gentleness, and
self-control. Paul's whole focus and desire, in other

words, was for the Lord *to totally inhabit and change his life.*

And that is exactly what happens when our greatest longing is simply *to know Him.* We begin to feel what He feels and naturally do what He would do; we begin to see other people through His eyes—or even perceive Him looking out at them through ours. And the more we get to know Him, the more the sense of His presence expands to fill the deepest part of our being.

Paul didn't say, "that I may know Him ... and then go try to please Him."

If you think about it, it's not unlike the relationship some of us might have with our spouses: over time, we internalize the essence of their thoughts and feelings and acquire a sense of their presence that never leaves us. Likewise, as we grow into the Lord year by year, we acquire an ever-deepening heart awareness of who He is, and we naturally and effortlessly experience the fruit of the Holy Spirit that he engenders in us as well.

And contrary to what I used to think, we don't ever graduate from knowing God to just serving Him or applying scriptural principles to our lives. After all, Paul didn't say, "that I may know Him…and then go try to please Him." He said,

> …*that I may know Him and the **power** of His resurrection.*
>
> Philippians 3:10 (Emphasis added.)

Today, the same power that raised Jesus from the dead is alive in us. So, as long as our gaze remains on the risen Christ, we have one hundred percent of His love, joy, and peace—one hundred percent of *Jesus Himself*—operating within us. And that means that each one of us is now free to know what Paul expressed as the sum total of all his desire: *the infinite joy of being in relationship with Christ Jesus and the experience of His resurrection power living and growing in us—into all eternity.*

But this is the covenant which I will make with the house of Israel after those days...I will put My law within them and on their heart I will write it; and I will be their God, and they shall be My people. They will not teach again, each man his neighbor and each man his brother, saying, "Know the Lord," for they will all know Me, from the least of them to the greatest of them...for I will forgive their iniquity, and their sin I will remember no more.

JEREMIAH 31:33–34

No longer do I call you slaves...but I have called you friends, for all things that I have heard from My Father I have made known to you.

JOHN 15:15

God Chose Me

CHAPTER 2

*[God] chose us in
Him before the
foundation of
the world,
that we should
be holy and
without blame
before Him in love.*

EPHESIANS 1:4 (NKJV)

God Chose Me

But Is That Really Fair?

*[God] chose us in Him
before the foundation
of the world, that
we should be holy
and without blame
before Him in love.*

EPHESIANS 1:4 (NKJV)

God chose us.

Which is to say, God chose *me*.

And God chose *you*.

Now honestly, what's your first response when you read those words? Not sure you understand? Feel like you don't deserve it? Wonder what God might be expecting in return? Or whether it's even fair for Him to be "choosing" someone in the first place?

For many years I agonized over those same questions: *Why did He choose **me**? And what about all the people He didn't choose? If He is really as loving and merciful as He's supposed to be, how can He justify singling out some people, and not others? How can that be fair?*

> *Why did He choose **me**? What about all the people He didn't choose?*

And then there was my secret fear that being one of God's "chosen" really meant I was expected to live up to a higher-than-average standard—that if I didn't somehow overcome my anger, pride, lustful thoughts, and selfishness, He would eventually run out of patience and throw the lightning switch. I shuddered, in fact, every time I read those words "holy and without blame," because it was as if He were saying, *I saved you, Daryl, but I don't like some of those putrid things I still see in your heart. And while it's true I'm merciful up to a point, you'd better get rid of that nasty stuff pretty quick, if you expect your salvation ticket to be worth anything at the pearly gates.*

I was so caught up in fear of God and questions about His fairness that I actually missed the enormous impact the liberating words of Ephesians 1:4 could have exerted on my life. Even after encountering the living God that day in the hospital, I continued to struggle—for years!—with the words, *He chose me.*

Until one day, sitting at my desk with my Bible open to Ephesians 1:4, rehearsing the old familiar question of how a just God could play favorites, I heard Him gently say to my heart, *Daryl, the reason I chose **you** was...to know Me. I began, out of habit, to protest, Yes, Lord, but what about...?* But He spoke a second time: *Daryl—wait. I'd like you to just accept what I'm saying for right now...and leave the rest to My righteousness.*

Then, as I glanced back down at the words which for decades had constituted a veritable barrier between me and the God of the universe, my eyes fell on two short phrases I had never really noticed before: *in Him...* and *in love.* And for the first time, I saw the essence of the message Paul had intended to convey: that it was solely out of His incomprehensible mercy and kindness—out of sheer love—that Almighty God chose to "insert" me into His beloved and perfect Son, Jesus Christ. And it is therefore *in Jesus*—not in or of myself—that God now sees me as holy and blameless.

> *He made Him who knew no sin to be sin on [my] behalf, so that [I] might become the righteousness of God in Him.*
>
> 2 Corinthians 5:21 (Personalized.)

Which means that the very extent of my former failure and sinfulness, rather than being a source of fear and alienation from God, is now the basis of my endless praise of His goodness. And therefore my growing awareness of my "lost-ness" produces a continual sense of awe and gratefulness toward God for being willing to extend such incredible compassion and mercy, even to such a one as me. *Me:* the one who wanted to be the richest man in the world and didn't mind stepping over others to get there. *Me:* the one whose marriage was in shambles. *Me:* the one who was worshipping everything else in the world, except God…while still managing to convince everyone, even myself, that I was a "good Christian." And finally, *Me:* the one who had spent the better part of a lifetime questioning God's fairness, instead of praising Him for His unfathomable goodness.

It's almost too humbling and wonderful to comprehend.

So, isn't it curious, in light of the astonishing news that God has chosen us, that our first response to the idea is so often uncertainty, questioning, and debate? As I have pondered this over the years, I have come to the conclusion that what keeps many sincere Christians from accepting God at His word must be both our pride at play...and God's enemy at work. For the evil one knows that if we begin to grasp the extent of God's love for us, as it's

It is in Jesus—not in or of myself—that God now sees me as holy and blameless.

revealed in Ephesians 1:4, we can never again be the same. But as long as he can convince us God expects something of us, or keep us sitting in judgment of the Lord's fairness, he can rob us of the whole new life God is waiting to give us—*in Christ.*

Not long ago, I was reminded of this as I was strolling down the crowded, colorful streets of Cabo San Lucas,

Mexico. All around me, tourists and locals milled their way through crowded shops and paused to savor the exquisite food and drink of the bustling cafés. Observing their smiling, suntanned expressions, one could easily have supposed their lives were free from all care. But as snippets of conversation drifted past and I began to study their faces more closely, it became obvious that the "fun" they were so passionately pursuing was merely superficial—just one more expression of lives wholly consumed by doing and acquiring and experiencing, yet nevertheless failing to find peace.

Not for the first time, I found it hard to hold back my tears, realizing once again that it is only because God chose me that I am now free from the endless rat race of self-fulfillment I witnessed on the streets of Cabo. I am a completely new person. I don't have to party to feel good anymore. I don't need tranquilizers to dampen feelings of guilt or fear of the hereafter. Because I am chosen, I now know a far different joy: one that doesn't revolve around leisure-time pursuits or depend upon circumstances playing out favorably, but which flows naturally out of the everyday reality of *Christ in me.*

Today, when I consider that, apart from Him, I would still be a slave of the devil—locked in a mental world of his deception and doomed to a hell of superficiality, meaninglessness, and despair—all I can do is weep with a shame and gratitude that has no end. For God *in love*—in His infinite mercy and compassion—didn't leave me, Daryl, in the miserable pit I had dug for myself, but instead chose—*chose!*—to lift *me* up and bless *me*, as Ephesians says, *with every spiritual blessing in the heavenly places in Christ* (Ephesians 1:3).

Today, when I consider that, apart from Christ, I would still be a slave of the devil, all I can do is weep with a shame and gratitude that has no end.

In view of that, how could I ever praise Him enough?

As for all those old questions about God's fairness…well, over the years they've simply evaporated in the ever-brightening light of *truly* knowing the Lord. After all, He is the God whose ways the whole of Scripture proclaims as *"blameless," "just,"* and *"unfathomable,"* and of whom Job says:

> *It is unthinkable that God would do wrong.*
>
> Job 34:12 (NIV)

These days, Ephesians 1:4 simply makes me want to drop to my knees and never get up. Furthermore, it is the verse in which my attraction to every other Scripture finds its source. For through this verse, God has continued to free me from my many misconceptions about Him, which the following chapters describe in more detail. And because of its message, that old "Uncle Sam" image of God which once plagued me has given way to a living, growing awareness of a love I simply can't describe.

All because of three priceless words:

*He chose **me**.*

God has chosen you from the beginning for salvation through sanctification by the Spirit and faith in the truth. It was for this He called you through our gospel, that you may gain the glory of our Lord Jesus Christ.

But you are a chosen people...that you may declare the praises of him who called you out of darkness into his wonderful light.

1 PETER 2:9 (NIV)

His Words ~
My Lifeblood

*This book of the law
shall not depart
from your mouth,
but you shall meditate
on it day and night.*

JOSHUA 1:8

CHAPTER 3

His Words ~ My Lifeblood

How Verses Become Who I Am

What do daily devotions and exercise have in common? Thankfully, not as much as I once believed.

Every morning I go jogging for about thirty to forty-five minutes. It keeps my body in shape and helps clear my mind for the coming day. As soon as my run is over, however, I'm off to the more pressing daily issues of running a business. For the remainder of the day, jogging is all but forgotten.

There was a time when I saw daily devotions in much the same way as my daily jog; if I could just find time to read my Bible and pray for twenty minutes a day, it would mean I was, spiritually speaking, in pretty good shape.

Trouble was, to the extent I let my self-discipline slip

I never thought that Bible verses were relevant to the practical matters of running a business, such as employee and customer relations, cash flow, or sales.

and didn't keep that twenty-minute appointment with God — which was more often than not — I felt guilty. Time and again, I would drag myself back to the old study routine, fearing if I didn't, it was evidence I wasn't really a good Christian. Any real passion on my part to *know God* through the Scriptures and prayer was sadly lacking.

You see, I thought the spiritual life was, for the most part, divorced from the everyday realities of work life. I would readily refer to the Bible when preparing a Sunday school lesson or counseling friends about their marriage, or on those occasions when I was assailed by serious doubts about my salvation. But I never thought that Bible verses were particularly relevant to the practical matters of running a business, such as employee and customer relations, cash flow, or sales. So once my devotions were over for the day, and the "real" matters of earning a living occupied my attention, I seldom gave any more thought to the morning's Scripture reading.

Then a number of years ago, as I was preparing to teach an in-depth study on the book of Joshua, a verse from the first chapter grabbed my attention. There, God tells Joshua:

> *This book of the law shall not depart*
> *from your mouth, but you shall*
> *meditate on it day and night, so that*
> *you may be careful to do according to*
> *all that is written in it; for then you will*
> *make your way prosperous, and then*
> *you will have success.*
>
> Joshua 1:8

I was intrigued. Joshua isn't in the middle of a spiritual retreat when God tells him this—he has just assumed leadership of the entire Hebrew nation. He is, you might say, just getting ready to go to work! Yet right in the midst of the enormous tasks and responsibilities which face him, Joshua is told to keep his thoughts continually focused on the revelation of God. By doing so, God promises, Joshua will be sure to receive the wisdom, clarity, and peace he needs to carry out God's will for his life, day by day, moment by moment, in every single situation—to be, by God's definition, truly successful.

As the Holy Spirit works through verses to conform our attitudes and priorities to God's, our lives effortlessly come to reflect the very things those verses are talking about.

In the years since that first encounter with the book of Joshua, I've discovered that what was true for him is also true for us. When we take God's words, in whatever form they come to us, and lay them continually before

Him *throughout the day,* desiring only to know Him and His will, the Holy Spirit opens our minds to understand those verses in connection to every situation we face. We begin to see our circumstances, responsibilities, and relationships through the eyes of God's Word instead of

through the fallen, darkened understanding of our human nature. So instead of just "studying" Bible verses, we actually experience the thrill of them coming alive in us.

As the Holy Spirit in us joins Himself to God's words in our heart, those words become the bridge for us to understand and experience the life of Christ—*the kingdom of heaven*—within us. They acquaint us with who Christ truly is and increasingly establish His character and nature in our lives. They articulate the wisdom we need for every situation and decision in life. And as the Holy Spirit works through them to conform our attitudes and priorities to God's, our lives effortlessly come to reflect the very things those verses are talking about.

> *For this reason we also constantly thank God that when you received the word of God which you heard from us, you accepted it not as the word of men, but for what it really is, the word of God,* ***which also performs its work in you who believe.***
>
> 1 Thessalonians 2:13 (Emphasis added.)

The wonder of this came home to me in a powerful way a few years ago, as I lay in a hospital room recovering from an emergency angioplasty. Noticing the intravenous bag suspended above my left arm, I turned my attention to the medication dripping steadily into my veins. Suddenly, I recognized that God had shown me a wonderful metaphor for the affect *meditating* has on our lives.

The substance flowing out of that bag into my veins was nothing short of life-changing. Imperceptibly, those drops were feeding and sustaining me, holding at bay the lethal poisons in my blood, enabling me to *live*—doing for my physical body what meditating does for our spiritual life.

Think of it this way: our mortal blood is full of the hellish germs of impatience, pride, bitterness, fear, and the need to be in control. And although nothing may trigger them when we are feeling strong and things are going our way, the moment we get news that our teenage son stayed out too late with his girlfriend, or our rent just went up, or our biggest customer terminated his account with us, those passions fly immediately into high gear. They take over our thoughts, emotions, and actions, and leave us powerless to suppress them. They are, quite simply, "in our blood."

But when Christ's life is energized in us through the steady inflow of His Word, Christ's perfect nature works through that Word to overcome our weakened, powerless flesh. So the same events or situations that once triggered our sinful human-nature blood now result in Christ manifesting His life through us. His reactions increasingly become our own, and we know the joy and freedom of experiencing His gospel at work in us, *the power of God for salvation to everyone who believes,* as Paul expresses it (Romans 1:16).

For example, say we're meditating on 1 Corinthians 1:2, *to the church of God...sanctified in Christ Jesus, saints by calling,* and we're focused on the reality that God sees us as His "saints." Then, if a customer blasts us because our company just bungled a job, or our spouse criticizes us for some inconsiderate thing we did, instead of feeling defensive and beginning to make excuses, we remain calm in the assurance of God's continuing love and acceptance, and are able to focus positively on how to resolve the problem at hand.

That's real freedom!

Needless to say, after experiencing such practical, everyday liberation from stress in my own life, I no longer think of devotions as a quick spiritual jog around the block—because that would mean being disconnected from God's words for the entire rest of the day. And being disconnected, in my experience, feels like hell.

On the other hand, thinking about the Lord *throughout* the day keeps me connected all the time to His wisdom, peace, life, and joy. And honestly, friend—*that* feels like a bit of heaven.

May your compassion come to me
  that I may live,
For your law is my delight...
It is my meditation all the day.

PSALM 119:77, 97

It is God who is at work in you,
both to will and to work for His
good pleasure.

PHILIPPIANS 2:13

Be renewed in the spirit of your
mind.

EPHESIANS 4:23

Wrapped in a Perfect Robe

I will rejoice greatly in the Lord,
My soul will exult in my God;
For He has clothed me with
the garments of salvation,
He has wrapped me
with a robe
of righteousness.

CHAPTER 4

ISAIAH 61:10

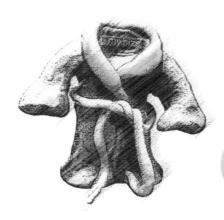

Wrapped in a Perfect Robe

More Than a Ticket to Heaven

I once asked a hairdresser, a Christian, what percentage of her clients she thought derived a significant portion of their identity and self-worth from the way their hair looked. She was thoughtful a moment, and then to my surprise replied, "maybe 80 percent." I then asked her if the same held true for her Christian clients. "Oh, yes" she said immediately. "In fact, with Christians, it's possibly even higher."

If what she says is accurate, most people, even among the ranks of believers, are suffering from a serious case of identity crisis. But perhaps we shouldn't be surprised. I mean, think about how easily we as Christians fall into the trap of comparing ourselves to others, even—or perhaps especially—to our brothers and sisters in Christ. How often does the limited insight we have into their lives become the benchmark by which we define our own personal worth? And how often are we devastated by the results, left to feel inferior to everyone around us, and worse yet, disappointing to God?

Most people today are suffering from a serious case of identity crisis.

Growing up, I often felt that way. I saw myself as inferior to everybody and everything. Because I was somewhat small in stature, I actually pumped weights in an effort to "bulk up"—thinking that would make me feel better about myself. But it didn't help. There was always someone else to compare myself to, and I always seemed to end up on the short end of things.

What I didn't realize then was that many, if not most, people suffer from the same feelings of inadequacy. We worry that we are less patient with our kids than others, or that we don't manage our finances as well. We assume the struggles of our private thought life are unique to us, and far worse than any waged in the minds of those we hold in high esteem. We wonder, too, what our spouses really think of us, and whether they would have married us way back when, had they known as much about us as they do today. And sometimes, even as adults, we continue to agonize over our relationship to our parents, believing they never really wanted or loved us, or that they wished we had never been born, or had been born the opposite sex.

The Lord never intended us to be "good enough" apart from Him.

Looking around, we see others leading apparently happy, productive lives, and we are left feeling that our lives produce little more than liability and failure. That we're never quite good enough. That we can never please everyone. That, when everything is said and done, we are simply...*inadequate.*

It's a painful reality that can become the driving force in our lives. But it's not what God intended for us at all. The liberating truth is, the Lord never told us we could be "good enough," apart from Him.

Listen to what Paul writes:

> *Not that we are adequate in ourselves to consider anything as coming from ourselves, but our adequacy is from God.*
>
> 2 Corinthians 3:5

Our adequacy...from God. Wow! When I first read those words after Dave's death, it was as if God had switched on a bright new light in my soul. Without ever realizing it, I had always gauged my own sense of worth and adequacy in terms of how well I could please and be accepted by others. Now God was telling me those things couldn't be achieved by me at all, but were gifts I had already received from Him.

I longed to believe this good news, but my own overpowering feelings of worthlessness still stood in the way. How in the world was I to have a sense of God's adequacy operating in my life, when for so long I had struggled to be, as Paul put it, adequate in myself?

You see, while I certainly believed I was saved by grace through faith, I had always looked at my salvation as a sort of "ticket" that would ultimately admit me to heaven. And while I acknowledged that believing in Christ had gotten me that ticket, I occasionally questioned whether I had actually believed hard enough for it to be valid when the time came. Having been taught that a legitimate ticket would be evidenced by good Christian conduct, I felt the need to reassure myself, and regularly took inventory of what I considered the do's and don'ts of the Christian life: *I don't smoke, I don't drink, I don't gamble or play around. I'm active in my church.* Still, I couldn't shake off the nagging worry that when my number was up, the ticket I was holding might not fit the slot of heaven's turnstile.

It never even occurred to me that salvation had anything to do with the here and now. I understood it to be essentially a matter of the afterlife. Hadn't I heard the question all my life, "If you died today, are you sure you'd go to heaven?" My main concern then on earth was proving to myself that my heavenly admission pass would indeed turn out to be good. So when, despite all my best efforts, I continued to feel inadequate—especially when I was criticized by others—it stirred up all the insecurity I felt about my eternal destiny.

2 Corinthians 3:5 had given me new hope, however, and I was hungry for the adequacy of God that Paul proclaimed. As a result, I continued to study and pray for more light; and ultimately, the Lord brought me to this verse in Isaiah, which forever transformed how I understood my relationship to Him:

> *I will rejoice greatly in the Lord, My soul will exult in my God; For He has clothed me with the garments of salvation, He has wrapped me with a robe of righteousness.*

Isaiah 61:10

Now, if I own a garment, it is tailored especially for my size and shape: it covers me, protects me, and is what others see of me. And that is how God describes my salvation: not as a "ticket," but as a robe of righteousness—of *worthiness*—that He has personally tailored and dressed me in!

The idea revolutionized my concept of God. If up to that time I had thought of Him as that stern Uncle Sam figure, pointing his finger at me from a poster on the wall, telling me to behave, now at last I began to see Him as He really is: tenderly taking the measurement of all my needs and fashioning a garment to be the perfect fit for me. As I look back, I have to say that my life was never the same again.

I realized salvation isn't some pie in the sky that kicks in on Judgment Day: it's the righteousness God sees me clothed in *today*. I don't need to wait and wonder whether I've really got eternal life; He's given me His life right here, right now. And I don't need to be frantically striving for perfection; He has already given me His own perfection. I don't even have to rely on the praise or approval of others to justify my existence or give my life special meaning, because God, the Creator of the universe, has clad me in His infinite and measureless worthiness.

A few years ago, I had the opportunity to share this with a dear friend who is an orthodontist. He had recently filed for bankruptcy and was struggling with the massive weight of believing he had let down his family—and God. Keenly aware of what it had cost the Lord to save him, my friend was overwhelmed by what he saw as his failure to "live up to his own side of the bargain."

But as I continued to share with him what the robe of righteousness had come to mean to me, a glimmer of understanding began to break through the drawn, strained features of his face. About six months later, he wrote to tell me the Lord had given him a wonderful way to remember what we had talked about.

"Every morning when I come to the office, before I start the day's work, I put on a white lab coat. All day long, it reminds me that I'm covered with the righteousness of Christ. It's a simple thing, Daryl, but I can't tell you how completely that little reminder has changed my life!"

Because we are wearing the robe of righteousness, God the Father is as pleased with us as He is pleased with His own Son, Jesus Christ!

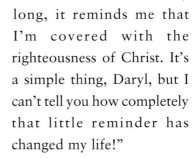

Just like my friend, every one of us can look at the robe we wear, every day, all day, and know that, as believers, our identity and self worth—now and for all time—are *in Christ*, in the very righteousness of God Himself. The Lord Himself put it on us, and He sees us wearing it every single day. And as incredible as it may seem, because we are wearing that robe, God the Father today is *as pleased with us as He is pleased with His own Son, Jesus Christ!*

Which means that from here to eternity, we're free just to say, *Praise God. Praise God. Praise God. Praise God....*

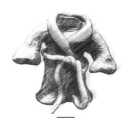

And this is His name by which He will be called, "The Lord our righteousness."

JEREMIAH 23:6

He made Him who knew no sin to be sin on our behalf, so that we might become the righteousness of God in Him.

2 CORINTHIANS 5:21

By His doing you are in Christ Jesus, who became to us wisdom from God, and righteousness and sanctification, and redemption.

1 CORINTHIANS 1:30

New Life
~
New Freedoms

No More Resentment

CHAPTER 5

*He who lacks these
qualities is blind
or short-sighted,
having forgotten
his purification
from his former sins.*

2 PETER 1:9

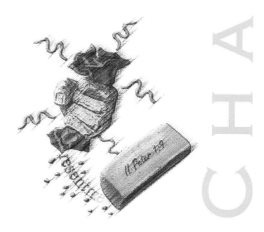

No More Resentment

Pulling the Plug on Anger and Bitterness

orgive and forget. As children, we hear it from our parents. As adults, we hear it from our pastors and marriage counselors and well-meaning friends. But it's not all that easy, is it?

Resentment and bitterness just seem to have a life of their own. I know, because for many years my inability to forgive others caused me untold struggle and despair. On the one hand, I was unwilling to forget some of the more horrendous offenses I had experienced, and I continued to rehash them in my mind, reliving the deep pain they had engendered. On the other hand, even when I tried to forgive what I considered "lighter" offenses, I often found they, too, exerted a stranglehold on my memory. In either case, just hearing the name of a person who had wronged me was enough to set off critical thoughts like fiery darts in my brain: *Look what they did...; If only they hadn't...; I should have...; Why didn't they just...?* And on and on and on.

No matter how I struggled to become a "good Christian," I remained a slave to the dictates of anger and bitterness.

These conversations in my mind were exhausting. No matter how hard I tried to suppress my negative feelings, they continued to eat away at me like a vicious cancer. At times, I honestly tried to forgive others, believing if I could just get ahold of myself, I would be able to let the thing go once and for all. But no matter how I struggled to "pull myself up by the bootstraps" and become what I

believed a good Christian ought to be, I remained a slave
to the dictates of anger and bitterness—until a passage
from 2 Peter gave me my first taste of freedom:

> *He who lacks these qualities is blind or*
> *short-sighted, having forgotten his*
> *purification from his former sins.*
>
> 2 Peter 1:9

Now, there was no doubt I lacked the "qualities" Peter
refers to here, qualities he lists in the preceding verses
and which include, among other things, agape love—the
unconditional love and forgiveness we associate with God
Himself. What took me by surprise was that Peter doesn't
say, "If you lack these qualities, then get busy and try
harder." Instead he says the root cause of our resentment
toward others is that we have failed to remember, or
have perhaps even denied, the immensity of our *own* sins,
from which God has completely cleansed us. In other
words, Peter claims, if we are still grappling with
bitterness and the inability to love and forgive others
who have wronged us, the core problem lies not with
them but with us. We have either not fully understood,
or have forgotten, that we ourselves have been forgiven
far more.

Unfortunately, we easily lose sight of that and start looking in all the wrong places to free ourselves from negative feelings. We try to block out bad memories or force-feed ourselves positive thoughts about the offender. Or we wait for him or her to apologize and change their ways, thinking that then we will be able to feel better about them. But Jesus compares such methods to those of the unjust servant in Matthew 18, who threw his fellow servant in jail for being unable to repay a loan of a hundred denarii (about two thousand dollars in today's terms), when he himself had just been forgiven the far greater debt of ten thousand talents (a whopping ten million!).

Only remembering God's forgiveness of us can free us to love and forgive others.

The unjust servant failed to recognize the enormity of his own debt, the cancellation of which had set him free to show mercy to his fellow. As a result, he felt constrained to demand full payment of what was due him. Likewise, when we fail to call to mind our own purification—when we feel that our sin is not as great as someone else's—we miss the renewed joy of contemplating Christ's love and forgiveness, and like the unjust servant, we too remain trapped in destructive emotions and our own fleshly need to "set things right."

We get caught up in the issue of what someone else has "done to us." It takes over our thoughts and gnaws on our nerves. We feel the pull to put down, avoid, or get back at the perpetrator, as our old nature shifts into gear. The last thing we want is to be in the presence of that other person.

But that's when we need to drop to our knees and fervently ask the Lord to reveal to us again both the abyss of our own sinfulness and the completeness of His forgiveness; because only remembering God's forgiveness of us can free us to love and forgive others.

> *For all of us have become*
> *like one who is unclean,*
> *And **all** our righteous deeds*
> *are like a filthy garment.*
>
> Isaiah 64:6 (Emphasis added.)

> *Whoever keeps the whole law and yet*
> *stumbles **in one point**, he has become*
> *guilty of all.*
>
> James 2:10 (Emphasis added.)

As far as the east is from the west,
So far has He removed our
  transgressions from us.

Psalm 103:12

I will forgive their iniquity, and their sin
I will remember no more.

Jeremiah 31:34

You see, the more we appreciate both the depth of our own depravity and the full extent of God's compassion, the more we can't help but also experience the natural outpouring of His love and forgiveness through us towards others: *We love, because He first loved us* (1 John 4:19). So we don't have to be irritated by the inconsiderate and unjust things people do to us, or constantly sucked into an endless whirlpool of bitter thoughts and painful memories. In fact, living in awareness of the magnitude of God's mercy, we find it's actually impossible to hold on to resentment and bitterness; His love and forgiveness of us are just too powerful. As Peter says: *His divine power has granted to us everything pertaining to life and godliness, through the true knowledge of Him who called us by His own glory and excellence* (2 Peter 1:3).

Even today, I continue to be in awe of the freedom this truth brings. For example, I own a franchising business, which provides support services to over 60 independently owned outlets around the nation. Because the royalty we receive from these franchises is based on their profits, not gross sales, it was troubling to discover recently that one company was submitting expenses not allowed under our procedural guidelines. In other words, the management of that franchise was lowering its profit for personal gain; and this in turn was reducing our rightful royalty.

When we live in awareness of the magnitude of God's mercy, we find it's impossible to hold on to resentment; His love is just too powerful!

What was my first reaction? Anger. Frustration. All the warning signs of resentment kicked into high gear, and peace long gone out the back door. *Why are they trying to take advantage of me,* I thought, *when I don't try to do that to them?*

But thank God, even as the weight of the offense was descending on me with its infernal stranglehold, a second question was already forming in my mind, *What in the world has happened to my peace?* And in the same instant I was reminded that, no matter how great a sum an associate might be trying to withhold from me, it was a paltry amount, compared to the enormity of what the Lord had forgiven me.

How many times like that, sensing anger and resentment suddenly coming alive again, have I recalled 2 Peter 1:9—and seen every bitter thought simply evaporate into a renewed understanding of all Christ has forgiven me! That's why I would eat a thousand copies of this verse, if doing so would keep me *remembering*. I'd buy that many Bibles, cut 2 Peter 1:9 out of each one, then sit at my desk and devour the whole batch.

That's how sweet this freedom tastes to me.

God demonstrates His own love toward us, in that while we were yet sinners, Christ died for us.

ROMANS 5:8

So, as those who have been chosen of God, holy and beloved, put on a heart of compassion, kindness, humility, gentleness and patience; bearing with one another, and forgiving each other, whoever has a complaint against anyone; just as the Lord forgave you, so also should you.

COLOSSIANS 3:12–13

He Will Make Me Know

*The secret of the Lord
is for those who
fear Him,
and He will
make them know
His covenant.*

PSALMS 25:14

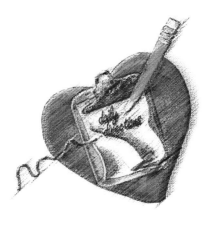

CHAPTER 6

He Will Make Me Know

Every Decision Made Easy

Have you ever stood before a difficult decision and wished with all your heart that you could somehow know—beyond the shadow of a doubt—just what the will of God really was?

You're not alone! Decision-making is potentially one of the most stressful aspects of the Christian life. For while we as believers would like to think that the choices we make are in accordance with what God desires, in reality it often seems difficult, if not impossible, to determine whether we are in fact "in His will," or simply yielding to the dictates of our own fear, impatience, and self-centeredness.

That's why for much of my life, decision-making caused me untold anxiety. Although I believed the Bible taught God did indeed direct us, the idea always appeared somewhat mystical, and it was unclear to me how He went about it, or what areas of life He actually involved Himself with. God's "leading," in fact, seemed obscure and unpredictable, for although at times I thought I knew what it was, at other times I simply didn't have a clue. And to top off my confusion, even when I did sense a clear inclination toward a particular decision, I ended up second-guessing whether God was really the One influencing me.

As a result, I was never totally at peace. At times I grew so desperate, I wished the Lord would just appear and tell me what I needed to know, because it didn't seem like there was any other way I would ever be 100 percent sure I was really following Him.

What a relief it was then, when two verses from Psalm 25 began to transform my whole understanding of how God leads us:

Who is the man who fears the Lord?
He will instruct him
   in the way he should choose.
The secret of the Lord is for
   those who fear Him,
*And He will make them **know***
   His covenant.

Psalm 25:12, 14 (Emphasis added.)

His covenant: the unique relationship by which God unites Himself to us and reveals His perfect will for our lives. And Psalm 25 says—definitively and unequivocally—that He will make us *know* it! Not that He will leave us hints and clues about His will, which we then need to piece together and "decode." Not that He "might" instruct us about what He wants for our lives, or that He will only do it occasionally, for the "big" issues. And not that it depends on us to find the pertinent Christian book or radio preacher to shed light on whatever our latest concerns or circumstances may be. But simply that if we fear Him—if our deepest inner longing is simply to know and experience God—He will make His presence and will *unmistakably clear* in regard to *every single thing* that concerns us!

We may be anxious about our child's relationship to the Lord, but unsure whether to even bring it up. Or we may be trying to cope with some troubling difficulty in our marriage, maybe even a situation that has gone on for years, which we don't know how to approach in a way that will avoid further argument and conflict. We may be confronting an underlying tension among our co-workers, or a disagreement between our kids. We're unable to discern where the problem is coming from or determine who is right, because whatever party we're talking to at the moment appears to have a legitimate concern; and the more we try to get to the bottom of the situation, the more convoluted and hazy everything seems.

> *If our deepest inner longing is to know the Lord, He will make His will unmistakably clear in regard to every single thing that concerns us.*

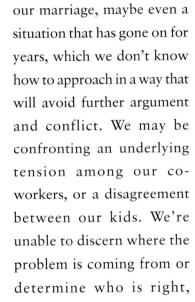

To all of this, Psalm 25 replies that God will instruct us in such a way that all doubt and ambivalence disappear. No more reading between the lines. No more guesswork. If we are willing to listen—*if we really want to know*—He will not fail to make absolutely sure we hear Him when He speaks.

Trouble is, we aren't always willing to wait for His voice, and in our impatience, we often make a crisis out of something the Lord does not. We start worrying our daughter is going to run off and marry the wrong boyfriend, or our teenage son is going to wreck the family car. Or we start stressing because the stock market is taking a plunge and the family budget is getting stretched. Like a drumbeat, the words *I've got to do something...* begin to pound in our anxious hearts, and we insist on running ahead and fixing things—right now.

God makes us know His will when He knows we need to know it.

Our anxiety or ambivalence, however, is a sure sign we have left off waiting for God's lead and are following our passions instead.

That's why it's important to realize that God makes us know His will *when He knows we need to know it.* So if we don't yet sense clearly and peacefully what to do, there isn't anything yet *to* do. Except pray. And if a situation arises that requires an immediate decision, we can be confident that God knows that as well, and will provide the counsel we need in plenty of time.

Not only that, we don't even have to guess at *how* He is going to do it, for regardless of how He speaks, God will always make sure we know it is His voice. He may bring a Scripture verse to mind, or speak to us through the wise comments of a Christian friend. He may put a strong desire into our heart to follow a certain path, or simply open or close a door. But however God's direction comes, we may be confident it will always be specific, unambiguous, and impossible to miss.

Moreover, and most importantly, it will always be accompanied by a deep, sure peace, which is the mark of His counsel. As Solomon wrote,

> *All [the paths of wisdom] are peace.*
>
> Proverbs 3:17

For God's peace—that quietness of spirit which is undisturbed by any fear, impatience, or ambition of our own flesh—is what distinguishes His voice from every other influence on our decision-making and confirms to us that one particular decision, and no other, is the Lord's leading.

What a freedom that is! Especially when we consider that our God is the Creator of the entire universe, and therefore uniquely able to oversee and bring complete harmony to *every* detail of our lives.

Take this recent example. Leaving my office to go home one evening, I noticed all the other rooms in the building were dark, except one. My son was working late. Passing his door, I slowed my feet. Should I stop, I wondered? He was facing an enormous crisis in his personal life; would this be a good time to have a talk?

God's peace—that quietness of spirit undisturbed by any fear, impatience, or ambition of our own flesh—is what distinguishes God's voice from every other influence on our decision-making.

My heart was torn. If I simply left the building, would I be letting him down? Mightn't a word from Dad be just the thing he needed tonight, to help straighten out the situation? Or would it be best to leave him alone just then, with his thoughts and, perhaps, with God? As the thoughts volleyed back and forth in my mind, my heart went down on its knees: *Lord, what would **You** have me do? What would You make me to know?*

Just as surely as if God's answer were in the soles of my feet, they slowly and deliberately turned toward the exit. Following their subtle but irresistible leading, I found myself heading out to the parking lot, the burden of my quandary left behind in the dimly-lit hall. I sensed God's gentle voice, as I strode out to my truck: *Not tonight, Daryl. This isn't the time.* With a relieved and joyful heart, I shifted into gear and turned the wheels toward home, once more praising God for the promise of Psalm 25:

He will make me know.

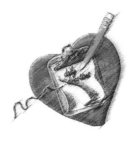

I will instruct you and teach you
in the way which you should go;
I will counsel you with My
eye upon you.

PSALM 32:8

You will go out with joy
And be led forth with peace.

ISAIAH 55:12

Wait for the Lord;
Be strong and let your heart
take courage;
Yes, wait for the Lord.

PSALM 27:14

When I'm Weak I'm Strong

CHAPTER 7

> *When I am weak, then I am strong.*
>
> 2 CORINTHIANS 12:10

When I'm Weak I'm Strong

God Doesn't Expect My Best

We live in a day when, outside of God's Word and the Holy Spirit, every influence on us stresses our need to be strong, in control, and solving our own problems. The cultural mantra, "Believe in yourself...you can do it!" bombards us daily: in the media, in our schools and places of work, and sometimes even in our churches. The expectations friends and family have of us, too, often find their source in the assumption that strength is necessary for success. Even our own pride demands that we remain independent and take care of ourselves.

So it's not surprising that for more than half of my life, I shouldered the constant stress of believing it was up to me to make something of my life: that while God provided opportunities, it was my responsibility to do something with them. My whole theology, in fact, was based on the false supposition that "God helps those who help themselves." So, I reasoned that as long as I kept doing my best for God, I could count on His grace kicking in at some point, if necessary, to make up anything lacking.

Unfortunately, I could never be certain about what my "best" really was, or how much God considered good enough. And believing God expected *anything* from me meant I continued to be anxious about my part of the deal. As a result, I was constantly taking the pulse of my own spiritual growth, along with trying to assess such things as: how much I was doing for God, how well I was raising my kids, and how often I was sharing my testimony.

So it isn't surprising that I was baffled, every time I read these words of Paul:

I am well content with weaknesses...for when I am weak, then I am strong.

2 Corinthians 12:10

The idea of being *weak* just didn't fit in with my "try harder" philosophy. What could it possibly mean, after all, to be a weak company president or manager...or husband? Didn't that go against all common sense? If God expected me to give Him my best, well then, what good would it do for me to become passive and docile?

The strength I was trying so hard to nurture was actually the root cause of all my stress!

Unable for many years to reconcile Paul's words with my concept of God's expectations, I simply

"filed" 2 Corinthians 12:10 in the back of my mind, along with several other similarly inexplicable verses. Then I forged on with what I considered to be the "life of faith:" struggling to act more "Christ-like" and exhibit more patience and "peace" in front of others. But my efforts only resulted in an even greater sense of frustration and powerlessness. Because although I didn't yet know it, the "strength" I was trying so hard to nurture was actually the root cause of all my stress!

As long as I remained focused on "ME"—my strength, knowledge, planning and forethought, my physical health, material success, and ability to be in control, etc., I bore the full weight of responsibility for every circumstance in my life. And I was continually anxious about my self-image, my marriage, my business, and most of all, my relationship to God. I thought I was living the "Christian life," but in reality, I was caught up in the snares of my own pride.

True, I knew the Scriptures said that Christians are to die to themselves, but I had always equated that with becoming totally inactive and living a "do-nothing" life. And I didn't see how I could expect grace from the God who "helps those who help themselves"—unless I myself was "doing" something first!

At my cousin's bedside, however, I had begun to experience a whole new God: One revealing Himself more and more, not only as loving and compassionate, but also as alive with resurrection power. And I was coming to understand that He was living in me—that

He had placed Himself there precisely so that I could experience Him, and so that He could manifest His joy and peace in me, in the midst of any and all circumstances.

So, at some point, Paul's words started to make sense to me, and I gradually came to realize I had been wrong all those years, thinking God expected me to give Him my best. The very opposite, in fact, was true: God calls our righteousness — our "best" — nothing more than *filthy rags!* (Isaiah 64:6 NKJV). Rather than asking for our "best," then, He wants us to recognize our *weakness,* because He

We are only free to experience God's strength to the degree we acknowledge we have none of our own.

knows that only when we are completely and consciously dependent on Him are we able to fully experience *Christ's life* coming alive in us. In other words, we are only free to become acquainted with God's strength to the degree we acknowledge we have none of our own.

Every time we begin to rely on the abilities of our own "flesh," we just crawl back under the loathsome load of our own impatience, selfishness, pride, and stress. But when we throw ourselves with abandon into the security of the Lord's sovereign arms, we immediately experience release from those intolerable burdens, and begin to understand what He meant, when He said,

> *Come to Me, all who are weary and*
> *heavy-laden, and I will give you rest.*
>
> Matthew 11:28

Then His thoughts, His plans, and His life become our own; and our hearts acquire the unshakable confidence that can only come from knowing God Himself is at the helm of our lives. Moreover, we are free to live in endless, stress-less joy, knowing that all the Lord will ever require of us is to admit what we, in fact, truly are: *weak.*

So if we're sitting in the office and bad news starts pouring in: the company is going to lose a major account; two of the top staff are at odds; the market just took another big plunge; we don't have to start stressing. Or if we're having trouble at home, because we can't seem to get through to our teenagers or we're struggling to communicate with our spouse, we can take it as a reminder that we are *weak*...and rejoice. Because precisely there, in the recognition of our personal powerlessness, we are at last delivered from the diabolical delusion that we control our own destiny, and are free instead to experience the joy of God manifesting *His* strength in our lives.

What's more, far from being the "do-nothing" existence I formerly imagined, the life lived in utter dependence upon God is the most powerful, effectual, freedom-filled life we could possibly experience—the very life that Christ Himself exemplified during His time among us on earth. And He is waiting at every moment to reveal it to us and in us, as He Himself testifies:

Far from being a "do-nothing" existence, it's the most powerful, effectual, freedom-filled life we can possibly experience!

> *The eyes of the Lord move to and fro throughout the earth that He may **strongly support** those whose heart is completely His.*
>
> 2 Chronicles 16:9 (Emphasis added.)

Sometimes, I'll admit, I forget. Things start to go wrong, and my blood pressure skyrockets, and that little voice inside my head goes off, saying, *Daryl, you need to do something here. You need to fix this. You need....*

But then my eyes catch a glimpse of a little sticker I keep nearby: a picture of a heart...on its knees. And it reminds me that there is absolutely no stress that kneeling won't alleviate. For the thousandth time, I can scarcely believe the relief that sweeps over me. Because even though it may still look like my whole world is going to hell in a hand-basket, I know the truth:

When I'm weak, then I'm strong.

The Lord is my strength and
  my shield;
My heart trusts in Him,
  and I am helped.

PSALM 28:7

The Lord will accomplish what
concerns me.

PSALM 138:8

"Not by might nor by power, but
by My Spirit," says the Lord of
hosts.

ZECHARIAH 4:6

CHAPTER 8

Chocolates From God

*Grace and peace
be multiplied
to you in the
knowledge
of God and of
Jesus our Lord.*

2 PETER 1:2

Chocolates From God

The World's Greatest Candy Store

eaven and hell, God and Satan: I've always believed in them. And although my concept of the Lord was for many years a largely negative one—being generated unbeknownst to me by His enemy—there was never any question that, given the choice, I would have much preferred to spend eternity in heaven rather than in that other place.

Nevertheless, because I equated being more committed to God with having less fun, I continued to entertain hope for a third option. You see, in my heart of hearts, I couldn't imagine that even heaven was able to outshine the simple pleasures of stalking big game or pulling in thirty-pound salmon. And I wasn't anxious to give up all that earthly fun just to spend a dubious eternity with a God I mostly feared. Harps and halos might have sounded prettier to me than fire and brimstone, but given my druthers, I would just as soon have stayed where I could be certain, from experience, that the fishing holes were good.

Right here on earth.

Not that I thought life was paradise: there were plenty of problems and painful circumstances to deal with, to be sure. But given that those could somehow be remedied, I figured I would be perfectly content to stay here, enjoying all eternity with my fishing rod. What greater happiness could there possibly be?

Then I encountered this very puzzling verse:

> *Grace and peace be multiplied to you in the knowledge of God and of Jesus our Lord.*
>
> 2 Peter 1:2

Now again, growing up, I had always understood the Bible to say that the degree of peace in my life was directly related to the amount I was obeying and serving God. So how, I mused, could just knowing more about Him translate into increasing grace and peace (which I interpreted as happiness) for my life?

Back then, it was my custom to spend an hour a day with *The Wall Street Journal* or *Field and Stream*, publications I found interesting and relevant, and which catered to my twin passions of business and sport. When it came to reading the Bible, on the other hand, I often made excuses, thinking I'd get to it as soon as I "had time." Frankly, reading the Scriptures seemed like just

Reading verses seems less like fulfilling an obligation, and more like eating calorie-free chocolates.

another burdensome daily duty, one more necessary ingredient of the Christian life to be checked off my morning to-do list. So I seldom got around to doing it. I was still operating under the misunderstanding that knowing God simply denoted knowing facts *about* Him. And since I saw God mostly as an exacting taskmaster, I was hesitant to know too much about Him, lest it make me even more uncomfortable.

But the day I stood by my dying cousin's bed, I felt a strange new attraction welling up within me: a powerful desire to know God *Himself*. And in the subsequent months, as He began, through His Word, to reveal more and more of His kindness and love, that desire continued to grow. Reading verses seemed less like fulfilling an obligation, and more like eating calorie-free chocolates. For the first time, I was truly hearing God's Word—and experiencing it! Like David, I was discovering that when we desire for the Lord to impress His Word into the depths of our hearts, it tastes *sweeter than honey* (Psalm 119:103).

I remember a particular occasion when this became vividly real to me. Our company was one year away from relocating its home office to a distant state, and long-time employees were struggling to meet the challenges of the transition. Some were bitter, finding themselves in the unexpected and difficult place of having to look for new employment. A cloud of gloom and anger hung in the air.

Rising from bed one morning, and contemplating the coming day's tasks in such an atmosphere, all I could think of was the secret dread I felt. "I just hate to go to work today," I confided to my wife. Nevertheless, I forced myself to my feet and headed for the shower. An hour later, however, as I stood, briefcase in hand, ready for work, Sherryl surprised me. "Daryl," she said, "the Lord has given me a verse for you: *'This is the day the Lord has made; Let us rejoice and be glad in it'* (Psalm 118:24)." Suddenly, standing in the doorway with her, I felt the tiresome burden of dread slip quietly off my shoulders, as the full impact of the Psalmist's words hit home: *This day hasn't fallen through the cracks of God's sovereignty. God's loving plan for me is as much for this day as it is for every other.*

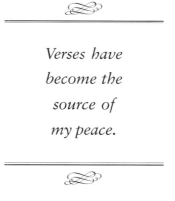

Verses have become the source of my peace.

In an instant, that realization completely changed how I saw my workplace, and I headed to the office in peace-filled, quiet confidence—not only that day, but for months thereafter. Never before had any magazine or newspaper had that effect on me! I had tasted another marvelous chocolate—roughly the equivalent of a five-pound bar of homemade fudge.

It's a typical example of what I have experienced again and again, as I have continued to study God's Word with a growing longing to know Him; every new bit of genuine revelation from that Word brings a corresponding freedom from bondage to the deception and despair of the evil one and deepens my yearning to know even more of the Lord.

So rather than keeping Him at a distance, as in the past, I now hunger for more and more of His presence. And rather than continually doing battle with a negative image of God, I experience a mounting contentment and joy permeating every area of my life. Like a kid in a candy store, the more verses I encounter, the more I crave! And as each year passes, my list of favorite chocolates just continues to grow, so that 2 Peter 1:2, as the Living Bible expresses it, now describes my heart's greatest desire:

*Do you want more and more of God's
kindness and peace? Then learn to know
him better and better.*

2 Peter 1:2 (TLB)

That's what verses have done for me: allowed me to know Him better and better, so much so that they have become the source of my peace—and far more relevant than any financial or sports journal could ever hope to be. Why? Because only the Lord knows exactly where I am living right at this moment: He knows every situation I face at home and work and church, and cares about every single detail that weighs heavily on my heart. So when I read His Word, He is able to speak to every aspect of my current situation and comfort me with the knowledge that He is always at hand: not to punish or berate me, but only to enfold me in His infinitely compassionate and secure embrace.

For instance, whenever the old familiar burden of my flesh begins to pull me down, and I get sucked into the hopeless task of suppressing all my petty, bitter, selfish impulses, it is the powerful truth of 1 John 4:4, *Greater is He who is in you than he who is in the world,* that enables me to drop to my knees and experience sweet relief.

And when I'm away from family members, rather than feeling inclined to beg, "Please, Lord, just be with them — and with me," the sweet savor of Hebrews 13:5, *"I will never leave you or forsake you," says the Lord* (NKJV), causes me to simply praise Him instead that He is *always* with them and me — at every time and in every place.

Finally, there's that most delectable of all treats, worth 20 pounds of Grandma's special recipe chocolate truffles: Proverbs 20:24.

> *Since the Lord is directing our steps,*
> *why try to understand everything that*
> *happens along the way?*
>
> Proverbs 20:24 (TLB)

It assures me I don't have to go looking for God's will, or wondering if and how I'll recognize His leading when it appears; the Lord is directing my steps, and that liberates me from the burden of agonizing over every little detail along the path.

That is immense freedom! And it's for every day and every situation of our lives.

I once shared this truth with the wife of a dear friend and former business associate. Her husband had left the business world and the two of them were spending the summer studying a foreign language in preparation for mission work abroad. Over the phone on one occasion, this dear lady confided how weary they had become of living out of boxes, in limbo between their former life and the new venture before them. Amidst tears of frustration, she exclaimed how glad they would both be when they finally arrived on the mission field and were again in God's perfect will.

Because the Lord directs my steps, that liberates me from the burden of agonizing over every little detail along the path.

To her surprise, I assured her that at that very moment—wearing only a bathrobe and confronting a living room piled high with packing boxes—she was every bit as much in God's perfect will as she would be when she reached her foreign destination. Her despair gradually gave way to relief and joy as we shared the precious and comforting words of Proverbs 20:24.

Praise the Lord!

These days, because of the incomparable sweetness I find in Scripture, those business and sports articles I used to devour don't hold much attraction for me; mostly, in fact, they just tend to create distraction and stress. On the other hand, I can never get enough of the Lord, because spending time with Him in His Word has the very opposite effect. *It* always brings a deep and satisfying peace.

And endless chocolates.

As the deer pants for the water
    brooks,
So my soul pants for You, O God.
My soul thirsts for God, for the
    living God.

PSALM 42:1–2

Because Your lovingkindness is
    better than life,
My lips will praise You.
My soul is satisfied as with marrow
    and fatness,
And my mouth offers praises with
    joyful lips.

PSALM 63:3, 5

Wisdom will enter your heart
And knowledge will be pleasant to
    your soul.

PROVERBS 2:10

God Only Gives Good Gifts

*If you then, being evil,
know how to give
good gifts to
your children,
how much more will
your Father who is in
heaven give what is good
to those who ask Him!*

MATTHEW 7:11

CHAPTER 9

God Only Gives Good Gifts

"Be Careful What You Pray for" Is a Line from Hell

*T*ry to imagine this:

A young mother stands sipping her steaming mug of freshly brewed coffee in the half-dark kitchen. It is early morning. The woman contemplates a blue plastic lunch box lying open on the cabinet before her. Last night her son Jimmy pleaded with her to pack his favorite foods to take to school today: a peanut butter sandwich, milk, and a bag of his favorite chips. The woman smiles to herself as she considers the request.

"I think a surprise menu is in order for lunch today," she murmurs, and slips quietly out the door into the back yard....

Later that day, in the bustling cafeteria, Jimmy spots an open seat and hurries over to it, plopping his unusually weighty lunch pail onto the metal table. "I wonder what Mom put in this thing," he mutters, flicking open the latch. Horrified, he gapes at the contents before him. There enshrined in blue plastic lies a small, dirty rock beside a writhing, agitated snake. A small note card to one side reads simply:

> *Enjoy your lunch, Jimmy.*
>
> *Love, Mom*

*   *   *

"Absurd!" you may be thinking. "Who would ever put a snake in their child's lunch pail?" Yet that is exactly the illustration Jesus used in the Sermon on the Mount when He asked,

> *What man is there among you who,*
> *when his son asks for a loaf, will give*
> *him a stone? Or if he asks for a fish, he*
> *will not give him a snake, will he?*
>
> Matthew 7:9-10

Jesus understood the struggle many people have coming to God with a request; the familiar maxim, "Be careful what you pray for," expresses it perfectly. It is not uncommon for people—even Christians—to fear that if they ask God for what they need, He may very well do something awful to them in the process of granting their petition.

They are unwittingly bound to an image of God as a disgruntled ogre who puts snakes in their lunch box and roadblocks along their path as a means of freeing them from fear and giving them the opportunity to develop patience and long-suffering.

Some people fear, if they ask God for what they need, He may do something awful to them in the process of granting their petition.

But that is a far cry from the God Jesus presents in Matthew,

> *If you then, being evil, know how to give good gifts to your children, how much more will your Father who is in heaven give what is good to those who ask Him!*
>
> Matthew 7:11

Jesus presents God, not as a stern, sadistic taskmaster, but as a loving Father who is ready at the first sign of our request, to reach for the wrapping paper. Jesus assures us here of the wonderful fact that our Father in heaven truly gives only the very best.

Jesus presents God, not as a stern, sadistic taskmaster, but as a loving Father who is ready at the first sign of our request, to reach for the wrapping paper.

Over the last thirty years I've heard countless people say to me, "Daryl, I'm afraid to pray, because of what God might do to me in order to teach me." But whatever fear we may have that God would harm or do evil to us in response to our prayers is completely eliminated by that one simple phrase, *what is good*. It reassures us that God will never put a snake in our lunchbox, and will never harm us as a result of our prayers. And just in case we have trouble understanding what God's goodness toward us consists of, Jesus relates it to something we can easily understand: our goodness to our own kids!

Who can deny the irresistible joy that wells up in our hearts, when we watch our young children excitedly ripping the bows and wrapping paper off long-awaited Christmas packages and hear their squeals of delight at the prizes tucked inside? Even though all my children are adults now, my wife Sherryl still takes painstaking care every Christmas to search out just the right present for each one; and as they unbox the gifts she has chosen, she derives genuine joy from observing their pleasure.

The source of our joy is not our external situation, but the life of Christ growing within us.

The amazing truth of Matthew 7:11 is that our Father in heaven looks on us the very same way we do our children when we give them a beautiful doll or a spanking-new, red fire truck to play with! And He is the One who lovingly packs every single "lunch box" we will ever open.

Of course, a healthy diet consists of more than Twinkies™ and potato chips. And sometimes even the best gifts in life appear at first to be daunting challenges. But when we are fully convinced that *all* God's gifts are truly for our good—that *in time* every one of them is destined to produce the good fruit of His Spirit in us— then even the most difficult circumstances cannot rob us of the joy of being His children. Because the source of our joy is not our external situation, but *the life of Christ growing within us.*

Paul says it this way:

> *We know that God causes all things to work together for good to those who love God, to those who are called according to His purpose. For those whom He foreknew, He also predestined to become conformed to the image of His Son, so that He would be the firstborn among many brethren.*
>
> Romans 8:28–29

So, because God in His goodness wills that believers become like His Son in all things, we can be confident that every time we lay our hearts before Him, He is already at work answering our prayers—by producing more of Christ's life in us. And more of Christ's life in us means we experience more of His unconditional love, joy, and peace that never waver, regardless of life's shifting circumstances.

Furthermore, since God's dealings with us are always completely good, each time we pray we know God is generating a first-rate, 100-percent-perfect response to all our needs. He never gives us lesser goods initially, later stripping us of them in order to grant us something "better." Rather, *every* gift He sends is—by definition— the *very best*. Because, as James put it, there are no "shades" of good with God:

> *Every good thing given and every*
> *perfect gift is from above, coming down*
> *from the Father of lights, with whom*
> *there is no variation or shifting shadow.*
>
> James 1:17

So we never need to fear that God will stick nasty surprises in our lunch box when we pray. And even if the world or the devil himself manages to slip in an unsavory circumstance from time to time, God will turn even that into the sweet delight of spiritual fruit. Matthew 7:11 assures us of this. It's like a personal note written by God to comfort our hearts in the midst of life's ups and downs, with His Fatherly love.

To me, it reads something like this:

Dear Daryl,

Think about how you love doing good things for your children. Then consider that you are my child, and that I—being God—have a far greater capacity to be good to you than you could ever be to them. That's why you can be sure I will always answer your prayers, and will do so by delighting you with gifts that are infinitely more suited to your needs than any you could possibly imagine giving to them.

Be at peace, therefore, my child—and never fear to ask me for all the things you need.

Love,

God

Now, I ask you: with a Father like that, why would we want to be anywhere else but in constant prayer before Him?

How great is your goodness,
Which You have stored up for those
who fear You!

PSALM 31:19

Surely God is good to Israel,
To those who are pure in heart!

PSALM 73:1

I walk in the way of righteousness,
in the midst of the paths of
justice:
To endow those who love me with
wealth, that I may fill their
treasuries.

PROVERBS 8:20–21

Surely goodness and lovingkindness
will follow me all the days of
my life.

PSALM 23:6

A Heart On Its Knees

Be anxious for nothing.

PHILIPPIANS 4:6

CHAPTER 10

A Heart On Its Knees

God Is Taking Care of Everything

*Be anxious for nothing, but in everything by
prayer and supplication with thanksgiving let
your requests be made known to God. And the
peace of God, which surpasses all
comprehension, will guard your hearts and
your minds in Christ Jesus.*

PHILIPPIANS 4:6–7

*D*o you struggle at times with worry and anxiety? I certainly do. I spent the better part of my life anxious about virtually everything you can think of: whether my business was going to grow or decline in a given year, whether my taxes were going to go up, whether I was being a good enough Dad to my kids, whether my health was holding, whether my relationship with God was what it should be....

That's why I find such powerful comfort and reassurance in the phrase, "Be anxious for nothing." Especially that one little word, "nothing." It really gets my attention and serves as a daily check on my stress. It has caused me literally hundreds of times to stop and realize that when God says we don't need to worry about life, He is referring to every single problem and situation we can possibly encounter.

To put it another way, God's use of the word "nothing" leaves out, well... *nothing*. And that means it includes everything!

So, for example, it includes our marriage, no matter what kinds of difficulties we face with our spouse, or how long those challenges have gone on. It includes our kids, whatever their relationship to the Lord, and whatever their daily circumstances may be—whether it's a child who is struggling in school, or a rebellious teenager, or a son-in-law out of work, or a daughter having trouble adjusting to married life. "Nothing" includes every one of those problems, as well as every concern we have about our church, our job, our health, or the people with whom we associate every day.

And since "nothing" includes every aspect of life, doesn't it also include all our past failures as a parent or a spouse? As well as the secret sins of our life that no one knows about except us? Furthermore, doesn't it include our entire existence—past, present, and future?

Taking it to the next level, what about the pace of our spiritual growth? Whether we are reading our Bible or witnessing enough, whether we're becoming more patient, or kind, or forgiving? Doesn't "nothing" include all those things too?

You see, as Christians, we can so easily begin to feel like a man on one of those old-fashioned railroad pump cars: sweating and stewing and straining hard, pumping up and down the rails in an effort to "follow the Lord" and be the better person we think He expects us to be. But Philippians tells 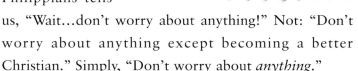 us, "Wait...don't worry about anything!" Not: "Don't worry about anything except becoming a better Christian." Simply, "Don't worry about *anything*."

Period.

What a relief it is to know that, while I'm heaving away on my pump car with sweat flying in all directions, God comes alongside in His gleaming locomotive and says, "Daryl, I see you wearing yourself out with effort and good intentions and even thinking it's all somehow for My benefit. But you've got the picture all wrong. You don't have to brave the elements, trying to pump your way down the track. I've already hooked you up to the engine. So, take a rest, and enjoy the scenery; I'm in the driver's seat now, and I'm already pulling you along."

Ask yourself, "Is there a parenthesis after the word 'nothing' that excludes the particular thing I am worrying about?"

It makes me want to fall down and praise Him forever for bringing me such incredible relief and freedom.

Well, that's all very nice, you may be thinking at this point, but what about the Christian life? Shouldn't I be trying my best to serve the Lord? Don't I need to be concerned about becoming a better example to my kids, or stepping up the pace of my spiritual growth? And what about all the times I've failed in the past? Shouldn't I be at least a little anxious that I might trip up again? Then too, what about my dear friend, who doesn't know the Lord? Or that kid of mine, who is always pushing the limits? And now that you mention it, Daryl, how about...? and fill in the blank with whatever tempts you the most to worry.

Then ask yourself, is there a parenthesis after the word "nothing" which excludes that particular thing?

How much unrest in our lives is really a result of having a pump-car mentality? Of not taking the word "nothing" at face value? How much peace are we missing by inserting a pair of brackets after that word and excluding whatever concern is currently facing us, when all we really need to do—all we can do, if the truth be known—is to get on our knees before Him. Call it yielding, or submitting, or a heart of soft wax, it's all the same: allowing God to be both the direction and the power of our lives, admitting we can't add anything to Him, but can only stay on our knees in the car and let Him be the conductor.

But wait, you ask, isn't that just a passive, do-nothing Christianity? Doesn't Jesus Himself speak against that kind of life, when he tells us to take up our cross and follow Him?

For much of my life, I thought so. I believed God's commands were laws I was expected to try my best (with His help) to obey. I therefore saw the Christian life as a sort of joint enterprise: part God, part me. If I just managed to do my share, He would give me the grace to make up the difference. To use the train analogy again, I figured He was out front in the locomotive, glancing back at me in the pump car now and then. Whenever He saw me running out of steam, He'd reach back and shoot a syringe of grace into my biceps, so I could go another mile. That was how I defined faith, in fact: simply believing He would never let the supply of grace completely run out, but would always be there in the nick of time with the next injection—so I

The only thing God expects us to "do" for Him is continually lay our lives at His feet.

could keep striving to fulfill my responsibilities as a Christian.

Unfortunately, such "faith" can run a person ragged! What a relief it was therefore, when my heart finally heard the Lord's gentle words, *Daryl, be anxious for nothing,* and understood that the only thing He expects any of us to "do" for Him is continually lay our lives at His feet. So at those times we are tempted to ask, *How should we be serving the Lord?* His voice says simply, *Kneel.* And if we are wondering how we can possibly change a difficult situation, He answers again, *Just kneel...and leave it to Me.* And when we have flung our hands up in desperation because there doesn't seem to be any light at the end of the tunnel, the reply still comes back the same, *Kneel,*

Moved forward by His wisdom, strength, and direction—apart from our efforts, plans, and agendas—we are, as God intended, truly at rest.

child, and find rest. You are safely on board, and the train is already moving toward its destination.

You see, every time we start assessing what we're doing to please God, we end up feeling like we're right back on the pump car—sweaty and stressed. Although we haven't actually left the train, and *the peace which passes comprehension* still surrounds us, our spiritual eyes are blind to it. On the other hand, every time we kneel, we become instantly aware of where we truly are: inseparably joined to grace—*Christ Himself*—aboard the train. And that knowledge fills us with an awe that simply increases our desire just to remain there in His presence. We see our lives being miraculously moved forward along *His* rails, by *His* wisdom, strength, and direction—and apart from *our* efforts, plans, and agendas. Then we are, as God intended, truly *at rest*.

Of course, in this life, we are never totally free from that old pump-car way of thinking. Even as I come to the end of writing this closing chapter, my human nature is already whispering, *Daryl, you haven't done enough yet. You've got to get going on the next book, and you've got to get it written a lot faster than you did this one. After* all, you're not getting any younger, and...." Just like the disciples besieged by wind and waves on the Sea of Galilee, I feel the raging waters of my perfectionist personality threatening to engulf me with all the things I "need" to get done to "please God." And all I can do is cry out with Paul,

> Who will set me free from the body of
> this death?
>
> Romans 7:24

But just as the sweat is beginning to pour off my brow and I'm wondering how in the world I'll ever get everything accomplished, Jesus comes alongside and silences the storm with one calm word, "Peace! Be still!" Then I'm reminded once again: *It's not when I'm in control that I'm strong. It's when I'm on my knees.*

That's good news! Jesus promises His rest to all who are weary and heavy-laden, and guarantees His peace to all who cast their cares on Him. And because we are on board the train—*in Christ*—we have access to that rest and peace twenty-four hours a day, every day, everywhere God's engine takes us. Which means we can live in total assurance that He is *always* in us, and that we are therefore partakers of *all* that He is.

Just for the kneeling.

And God is able to make all grace abound to you, so that in all things at all times, having all that you need, **you will abound** in every good work.

2 CORINTHIANS 9:8 (NIV Emphasis added.)

Delight yourself in the Lord;
And He will give you the desires
  of your heart.
Commit your way to the Lord,
Trust also in Him, and He will do it....
Do not fret; it leads only to
  evildoing....
Those who wait for the Lord, they
  will inherit the land.

PSALM 37:4–5, 8–9

Come to Me, all who are weary and heavy-laden, and I will give you rest.

MATTHEW 11:28

Cease striving, and know that I am God.

PSALM 46:10

ONE LAST WORD...

*What then does it mean
to know the God
who chose us?*

In essence, it means to experience LIFE—the very life of Christ Himself. To have His emotions, His thoughts, His compassion, and His unconditional love flowing through every fiber of our being. And to increasingly experience within ourselves everything that Christ is by His very nature: love, joy, peace, patience, kindness, goodness, faithfulness, gentleness, self-control, wisdom, understanding... *everything He is.*

For knowing God is not so much something we do, such as trying to imitate Christ or somehow apply His Words to our daily conduct. But it is yielding our hearts completely to the Lord and experiencing as a result how the qualities of His new nature take root and grow in our lives, fulfilling *all* He asks us to obey through the divine power of God Himself—the power He has placed in every Christian heart: *Christ in you, the hope of glory* (Colossians 1:27). And because that power is the same which raised Christ from the dead, when we desire the Lord to manifest it in us, there is no problem, circumstance, or aspect of our human nature—no force on earth, in fact— that can possibly stop Him from doing so.

As we grow in the true knowledge of God through His Word, He multiplies His grace and peace in our lives and gives us *everything pertaining to life and godliness,* so that we actually become *partakers of the divine nature* (2 Peter 1:2–4). He frees us from the burden of our self-imposed, futile attempts to "serve" and "please" Him, and instead manifests His own life in and through us. Our new life in the Spirit appears as naturally and effortlessly as our old self-life once did, with its anger, fear, and impatience. And because we experience the sweetness of the Lord's attitudes and feelings operating within us rather than the self-centered and sin-laden inclinations of our own flesh, our hearts are increasingly filled with delight and the longing to experience Him even more. Then, for the first time, our lives give true testimony to what Jesus meant, when He said,

> *Take My yoke upon you and learn*
> *from Me, for I am gentle and humble*
> *in heart, and you will find **rest** for*
> *your souls.*
>
> Matthew 11:29 (Emphasis added.)

This *rest*, my friend, is the sum total of the Christian life: Christ living and manifesting Himself in us. It is eternal life—not some hoped-for pie in the sky or biblical cliché, but perfect freedom—starting right here, right now. We experience it anew every time we come to the end of ourselves, when we truly recognize our own weakness, and when we desire *Christ's* life instead of our own.

Do you want to experience God like that? *Then tell Him so.* And He will surely make it happen. Once again— when your heart's desire is to *just...know...Him.*

*Behold, I stand at the door and knock;
if anyone hears My voice and opens
the door, I will come in to him and
will dine with him, and he with Me.*

REVELATION 3:20

*I came that they may have life, and
have it abundantly.*

JOHN 10:10

*Whoever drinks of the water that I
will give him shall never thirst; but
the water that I will give him will
become in him a well of water
springing up to eternal life.*

JOHN 4:14

*You will seek Me and find me when
you search for Me with all your heart.*

JEREMIAH 29:13

ENVIRONMENT CONTROL ™

P.O. Box 2000
Hayden, ID 83835-2000
Phone: (208) 772-8200
Fax: (208) 772-6045
www.environmentcontrol.com

It's About Lives Ministries is an extension of the spiritual influence that is woven through every aspect of Environment Control and was created in 1999 in response to the growing number of inquiries from the Church at large. *It's About Lives* provides materials for Christians desiring to experience the truth of God's Word more fully in their career, marriage, and family life. To order additional "Kneeling Heart" stickers or other audio, video, and print resources, visit us online at *www.itsaboutlives.org.*

It's About Lives Ministries
P.O. Box 3108
Hayden, ID 83835-3108
Phone: (208) 772-4256
Fax: (208) 772-6045
Email: lives@environmentcontrol.com

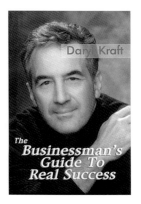

Don't be fooled by its title—this intriguing biography is for everyone! Beginning with Daryl's early struggles as a stressed-out, perfectionist businessman, the book moves quickly to the event that turned his understanding of the Christian life—at home and in the workplace—upside down. A compelling story, deeply yet simply insightful; a must read for every man or woman who has wrestled with the question: How can I ever do enough to please God?

Written specifically for career people, with topics like honesty, employee relations, handling complaints, and making decisions, this soon-to-be-released volume addresses fundamental issues Christians face every day on the job. In it, Daryl shares the enormous peace and freedom a growing understanding of Christ's presence within him has brought to his workplace over the last 25 years, while real-life stories richly illustrate his firm conviction that, for believers, true success and ministry in the workplace depend on just one essential element: a *pure heart*.